'You will hear it for yourselves, and it will surely fill you with wonder.'

MARCO POLO
Born 1254, Republic of Venice
Died 1324, Republic of Venice

Marco Polo left Venice in 1271 and spent twenty-four years in
Asia, where he became an important agent for Kublai Khan
and made many journeys through the Mongol Empire. On
his way home in 1291, he accompanied a diplomatic mission
that sailed on a fleet of junks via Sumatra, Sri Lanka and
India to the Persian Gulf. He wrote his famous *Travels*, from
which this selection is taken, while in prison in Genoa.

MARCO POLO IN PENGUIN CLASSICS
*The Travels*

# MARCO POLO

## *Travels in the Land of Serpents and Pearls*

*Translated by*
Nigel Cliff

PENGUIN BOOKS

PENGUIN CLASSICS

Published by the Penguin Group
Penguin Books Ltd, 80 Strand, London WC2R ORL, England
Penguin Group (USA) Inc., 375 Hudson Street, New York, New York 10014, USA
Penguin Group (Canada), 90 Eglinton Avenue East, Suite 700, Toronto, Ontario,
Canada M4P 2Y3 (a division of Pearson Penguin Canada Inc.)
Penguin Ireland, 25 St Stephen's Green, Dublin 2, Ireland
(a division of Penguin Books Ltd)
Penguin Group (Australia), 707 Collins Street, Melbourne, Victoria 3008, Australia
(a division of Pearson Australia Group Pty Ltd)
Penguin Books India Pvt Ltd, 11 Community Centre, Panchsheel Park,
New Delhi – 110 017, India
Penguin Group (NZ), 67 Apollo Drive, Rosedale, Auckland 0632, New Zealand
(a division of Pearson New Zealand Ltd)
Penguin Books (South Africa) (Pty) Ltd, Block D, Rosebank Office Park,
181 Jan Smuts Avenue, Parktown North, Gauteng 2193, South Africa

Penguin Books Ltd, Registered Offices: 80 Strand, London WC2R ORL, England

www.penguin.com

This selection published in Penguin Classics 2015
002
Translation copyright © Nigel Cliff, 2015
The moral right of the translator has been asserted

Set in 10/14.5 pt Baskerville 10 Pro
Typeset by Jouve (UK), Milton Keynes
Printed in Great Britain by Clays Ltd, St Ives plc

A CIP catalogue record for this book is available from the British Library

ISBN: 978-0-141-39835-8

www.greenpenguin.co.uk

## Travels in the Land of Serpents and Pearls

When the traveller leaves the island of Ceylon and sails westwards for about sixty miles he comes to the great province of Maabar, which is called Greater India. It is indeed the best of the Indies and forms part of the mainland. You should know that there are five kings in this province who are all brothers by birth; and we will tell you about each one in turn. You can also take my word for it that this province is the richest and most splendid in the whole world. And I will tell you why.

Now you should know that at this end of the province one of these brothers, Sundara Pandya Devar by name, is king. Fine pearls of great size and beauty are found in his kingdom; for the fact is that most of the world's pearls and precious stones are found in Maabar and Ceylon. And I will tell you how these pearls are found and gathered.

Now you should know that in this sea there is a gulf between the island and the mainland; and across this entire gulf the water is no more than ten or twelve paces deep, while in some places it is no more than two paces deep. It is in this gulf that the pearls are gathered, and I will tell you how. A group of merchants will enter into partnership and form a company, and they will take a large ship specially fitted out for the purpose on which each will have his own room equipped and furnished for his use with a tub full of water and other necessities. There are many of these ships, for there are many merchants engaged in this type of fishing and they form numerous companies. The merchants who are associated together on one ship will also have several boats to tow the ship through the gulf. And they hire many men, giving them a fixed sum for the month of April and the first half of May, or as long as the fishing season lasts in this gulf.

These merchants take their big ships and small boats out into the gulf from the month of April till mid-May. They make for a place on the mainland called Bettala, this being where the greatest concentration of pearls is found. From here they head out to sea, sailing due south for sixty miles, and there they cast anchor. Then they go out in the little boats and begin to fish in the following manner. The men in the little boats, who have been hired by the merchants, jump overboard and dive into the water, some descending four or five paces or even twelve depending on the depth of the water in each spot. They stay underwater as long as they can. When they can hold out no longer they come to the surface and rest for a moment before once more diving to the bottom; and they continue in this way all day long. When they reach the seabed they find a type of shellfish called sea oysters, and they bring them to the surface in little net bags tied to their bodies. In these oysters are found pearls, both big and small and of every variety. The shells are split open and put into the tubs of water that are carried on the ships as mentioned, because the pearls are embedded in the flesh of the shellfish. As it soaks in water in these tubs, the flesh decomposes and rots until it resembles the white of an egg; it then floats to the surface while the clean pearls remain at the bottom.

This is how the pearls are gathered; and the quantities found are beyond all reckoning. For you should know that pearls from this gulf are exported through-out the world, because they are mostly round and lustrous. I can also tell you that the king of this king-dom receives a substantial duty on them, amounting to an enormous sum in revenue. The merchants pay the following duty on the pearls. First of all they pay a tenth to the king. Then they give some to the man who charms the fish so that they do not do harm to the divers who go underwater to find the pearls; they give him one in twenty. These men are called Brah-mins and only charm the fish by day; at night they break the charm so the fish are free to do as they please. I can also tell you that these Brahmins are experts at charming every kind of creature, including all the birds and all the animals.

We have now told you how the pearls are found. And I give you my word that as soon as the middle of May comes round the fishing stops, because these shellfish – I mean the ones that produce pearls – are no longer found here. Yet it is true that about 300 miles away they are found from September to mid-October.

I can also tell you that in this whole province of

Maabar there is no need of tailors or needleworkers to cut or stitch clothes, because all the people go naked all year round. For I assure you that their weather is temperate at all seasons – which is to say it is never cold or hot – and so they always go naked, except for their private parts, which they cover with a scrap of cloth. The king goes round like the others, except for certain royal ornaments that I will describe to you. You may depend on it, then, that their king goes stark naked save that he covers his private parts with a beautiful cloth and wears round his neck a full collar so crammed with precious stones – rubies, sapphires, emeralds and other brilliant gems – that it is undoubtedly worth a fortune. He also has round his neck a thin silk cord that hangs down his chest to the length of a pace; and on this cord are strung very large, fine pearls and immensely valuable rubies, altogether 104 in number. I will tell you why there are 104 stones and pearls on this necklace. You may depend on it that he wears these 104 gems because every day, morning and evening, it falls to him to recite 104 prayers in honour of his idols, as ordained by their faith and customs and as practised by the kings who preceded him and who handed down the obligation to him. And this is the reason why the king wears these 104 gems round his neck. The prayer simply consists of the words '*Pauca, Pauca, Pacauca.*'

Let me further tell you that the king also wears, at three points on his arms, gold bracelets crammed with precious stones and pearls of great size and value. And let me add that this king likewise wears, in three places round his legs, gold bracelets crammed with opulent pearls and gems. I will tell you, too, that this king wears such beautiful pearls and other jewels on his toes that it is a marvellous sight to see. What else shall I tell you? You may take my word for it that this king wears so many gems and so many pearls that their value easily exceeds that of a substantial city; in fact there is no one who could reckon or estimate the great sum that these jewels worn by the king are worth. And no wonder he has as many jewels as I have said; for I assure you that all these precious stones and pearls are found in his kingdom.

Let me tell you something else. No one is allowed to take out of his kingdom any large and valuable gem, nor any pearl that weighs half a *saggio* or more. In fact several times a year the king issues a proclamation across his kingdom to the effect that all who possess fine pearls and precious stones must bring them to the court, and that in return he will give twice their value. It is the custom of the kingdom to pay double the value of all precious stones. So when merchants or other people have any of these precious stones and pearls, they readily take them to the court because they are well paid. And this is how this king comes to have so much wealth and so many precious stones.

Now I have told you about this. So next I will tell you about some other wonderful things.

I give you my word that this king has at least 500 wives or concubines. For I assure you that the moment he lays eyes on a beautiful woman or girl, he wants her for himself. On one occasion this led him into the shameful behaviour I will describe to you. Let me tell you that this king caught sight of a very beautiful woman who happened to be his brother's wife. And he took her from him and kept her for himself. His brother, who was a wise man, patiently bore his wrong and did not quarrel with him; and this was why. Despite his forbearance he was repeatedly on the brink of making war on him, but their mother would show them her breasts, saying, 'If you fight with each other I will cut off these breasts that suckled you.' And so the trouble was averted.

I will tell you yet another thing about this king that is truly to be marvelled at. I assure you that this king has large numbers of faithful followers who conduct themselves in the following way. The fact is that they declare themselves to be his followers in this world and the next. I will tell you more about this great wonder. These followers wait on the king at court; they go riding with him; they hold positions of great trust in his service. Wherever the king goes these barons accompany him, and they exercise high authority throughout the kingdom. And you should know that when the king dies and his body is burned in a great fire, then all these barons who were his faithful followers as I have told you above fling themselves into the fire and burn with the king in order to keep him company in the next world.

I will also tell you about a custom that prevails in this kingdom. The fact is that when a king dies leaving a great treasure, the sons who survive him would not touch it for anything in the world. For they say, 'I have the whole of my father's kingdom and all his subjects; surely I can find ways to profit from it as my father did.' Consequently the kings of this kingdom never touch their treasure but hand it down from one to another, each making his own fortune. And this is why this kingdom has such a titanic store of treasure.

Let me tell you next that this country does not breed horses. Consequently the entire annual revenue, or the greater part of it, is swallowed up by the purchase of horses; and I will tell you how this comes about. You may take my word for it that the merchants of Hormuz, Kish, Dhofar, Shihr and Aden – all provinces where chargers and other horses are plentiful – as I was saying, the merchants of these provinces buy up the best horses, load them on to ships and take them to this king and his four brothers, who are also kings. They sell each one for no less than 500 *saggi* of gold, which is worth more than 100 silver marks. And I assure you that this king buys no fewer than 2,000 of them every year and his brothers as many more. And by the end of the year not one of them has 100 left. They all die, because these people have no farriers and no idea how to care for them, so ill-treatment kills them off. And you can take it from me that the merchants who export these horses neither bring farriers with them nor allow any to come here, because they are only too glad for these kings' horses to die off in large numbers.

Let me move on to yet another custom of this kingdom, which I will describe to you. When a man has committed a crime that warrants the death sentence and the king has decreed his execution, the condemned man declares that he wishes to kill himself in honour and adoration of such-and-such an idol. The king replies that he approves of this. Then all the relatives and friends of the man who must kill himself take him and sit him in a chair and give him twelve swords or knives, and they carry him around the city proclaiming at every step, 'This brave man is going to kill himself out of devotion to such-and-such an idol.' They carry him like this round the whole city, and when they reach the place of execution the condemned man takes two of the knives and cries out loud, 'I kill myself for the love of such-and-such an idol!' Having uttered these words, at one stroke he thrusts the knives into his thighs. Then he thrusts two into his arms, two into his stomach, two into his chest and so on until he has stuck them all in his body, at every stroke calling out, 'I kill myself for the love of such-and-such an idol!' When all the knives are stuck in him, he takes a two-handled knife like those used for making hoops and holds it against the nape of his neck; then, jerking it violently forward, he severs his own neck, for the knife is razor sharp. And when he has killed himself his relatives burn his body amid great rejoicing.

I will go on to tell you about yet another custom of this kingdom. When a man is dead and his body is being burned, his wife flings herself on to the fire and lets herself burn with her husband out of love for him. The women who do this are highly praised by all. And believe me when I say that many women – though not all – do as I have told you.

I can also tell you that the people of this kingdom worship idols. Most worship the ox, because they say that an ox is a very good thing. None of them would eat beef for anything in the world, nor kill an ox on any account. I should tell you that there is a race of men among them called *gavi* who do eat beef, but even they would not dare kill an ox. Instead, when an ox dies of natural causes or gets killed by accident, these *gavi* whom I have mentioned eat it. And let me add that they daub their houses all over with ox dung.

I will move on to yet another custom of theirs, which I will describe to you. You should know that the king and the barons and all the other people sit on the earth. When asked why they did not seat themselves more honourably, they replied that it was honourable enough to sit on the ground since we are made of earth and to the earth we must return, from which it follows that no one can honour the earth too highly and no one should scorn it.

I can also tell you that these *gavi* – that is, that entire race of people who eat cattle when they die a natural death – are the same people whose ancestors killed Messer St Thomas the Apostle long ago. Let me tell you another thing, too: of all those of this tribe called *gavi*, none have been able to enter the place where the body of Messer St Thomas lies. For the fact is that ten men would not be able to cling on to one of these *gavi* in the presence of the holy body. I will go further: twenty or more men could not drag one of these *gavi* into the place where the body of

Messer St Thomas lies, because the place will not receive them by virtue of the holy body.

No grain grows in this kingdom with the sole exception of rice. And I will tell you an even stranger thing that is well worth relating. You should know that if a prize stallion mounts a prize mare, their offspring is a stunted colt with its feet askew that has no value and cannot be ridden.

I can also tell you that these people go into battle stark naked and armed only with a lance and shield. Far from being valiant or battle-hardened, they are mean-spirited cowards. They do not kill any animals or other living creatures; if they wish to eat the flesh of a sheep or any other beast or bird they have it slaughtered by Muslims or others who do not follow their faith or customs.

Let me tell you about another of their customs. All of them, men and women, bathe from head to toe in water twice a day – that is, morning and evening. They would neither eat nor drink without washing, and anyone who fails to wash himself twice a day is considered a heretic, much as we think of the Paterins. You should also know that in eating they use only the right hand; they never touch food with their left hand. Everything clean and pleasant they do and touch with the right hand, for the left hand is reserved for unpleasant and unclean necessities like wiping the nostrils, anus and suchlike. Another thing: they drink only from tankards, each from his own; for no one would drink from another's tankard. And when they drink they do not put the tankard to their lips but, holding it up high, pour the drink into their mouth. On no account would they touch the tankard with their lips or give it to a stranger to drink from. But if a stranger is thirsty and has not got his own tankard with him they pour the wine or other beverage into his palms and he drinks from them, making a cup of his own hands.

I can also tell you that harsh justice is administered in this kingdom to murderers, thieves and all other criminals. And as for debts, the following laws and procedures are observed among them. If a debtor who has been repeatedly asked by his creditor to pay a debt keeps on fobbing him off day after day with promises, and the creditor is able to get hold of him in such a way that he can draw a circle around him, the debtor cannot leave that circle until he has satisfied the creditor or given him a lawful and binding pledge that the debt will be discharged in full that very day. Otherwise, if the debtor ventured to leave the circle without paying the debt or pledging that the creditor would be paid the same day, he would incur the penalty of death for violating natural law and the justice established by the king. And Messer Marco saw this done in the case of the king himself. For it happened that the king was indebted to a certain foreign merchant for some goods he had had from him, and though the merchant had repeatedly petitioned him he kept on postponing the settlement date on the grounds of inconvenience. This delay was damaging him by blighting his business, so one day he made himself ready while the king was out riding and all at once drew a circle on the ground round him and his horse. When the king saw this, he reined in his horse and did not move from the spot until the merchant had been satisfied in full. When some bystanders saw this they exclaimed in astonishment, 'See how the king obeys the law!' And the king replied, 'Should I, who established this just law, break it because it goes against me? No, I more than anyone am obliged to observe it.'

I can further tell you that most of these people abstain from drinking wine. A man who drinks wine is disqualified from acting as a witness or guarantor, as is one who sails the seas; for they say that a man who goes to sea must be a desperado, and so they reject him and discount his testimony. On the other hand, you should know that they do not regard any form of sexual indulgence as a sin.

The climate is amazingly hot, which explains why they go naked. There is no rain except in the months of June, July and August; and were it not for the rain that comes during those three months and freshens the air, the heat would be so oppressive that no one could endure it. But thanks to this rain the heat is moderated.

I can also tell you that among these people there are many experts in the field of physiognomy – that is, the study of men and women's characters and whether they are good or bad. They ascertain this merely by looking at the man or woman. They are also expert at divining the meaning of encounters with birds or beasts. They pay more attention to omens than any other people in the world, and they are better than any others at telling good omens from bad. For let me tell you that when a man sets out for some destination and happens along the way to hear someone sneeze, he immediately sits down on the road and will not budge. If the sneezer sneezes again, he gets up and continues on his way; but if he sneezes no more, he abandons his journey and turns back for home.

Likewise they say that for every day of the week there is one unlucky hour, which they call *choiach*. So, on Monday it is the hour after seven in the morning, on Tuesday after nine, on Wednesday the first hour after noon, and so on for each day throughout the year. They have recorded and defined all these things in their books. They tell the hour by measuring the length of a shadow in feet – that is, a man's shadow. So, on such-and-such a day, when a man's shadow reaches seven feet long in the opposite direction to the sun, then it will be the hour of *choiach*. And when this measurement changes, whether becoming longer or shorter (for as the sun rises the shadow shortens and as it sinks the shadow lengthens), then it is no longer *choiach*. On a different day it will be *choiach* when the shadow reaches twelve feet long; and when this measure passes, then *choiach* will likewise be over. They have set down all these things in writing. And you must know that during these hours they steer clear of trading or doing any kind of business. So two men may be in the middle of bargaining together when someone steps into the sunlight and measures the shadow; and if it is on the cusp of that day's hour, according to what is laid down for the day, he will at once say to them, 'It is *choiach*. Stop what you are doing.' And they will stop. Then he will take a second reading and finding that the hour is past will say to them, '*Choiach* is over. Carry on.' They have these calculations at their fingertips; for they say that if anyone strikes a bargain during these hours he will never profit by it but will find it turns out badly for him.

Again, their houses are infested with certain animals called tarantulas that run up the walls like lizards. These tarantulas have a poisonous bite and cause great pain if they bite a man. They make a sound as if they are saying '*Chis!*' and this is their cry. These tarantulas are taken as an omen in the following way: if some people are doing business in a house infested with these tarantulas and a tarantula utters its cry within their hearing, they check its position relative to each merchant, whether buyer or seller – in other words, whether it is to the left or right, in front or behind, or overhead – and according to the direction they know whether its significance is good or bad. If good, the bargain is struck; if bad, it is called off. Sometimes it augurs well for the seller and ill for the buyer, sometimes ill for the seller and well for the buyer, and sometimes well or ill for both; and they modify their actions accordingly. They have learned these things from experience.

I can also tell you that as soon as a child is born in this kingdom, whether boy or girl, the father or mother immediately has a written record made of his nativity – that is, the day, month, lunar cycle and hour of birth. They do this because they always act on the advice of astrologers and diviners who are well versed in enchantment and magic and geomancy. And some of them, as I have told you, also know astronomy.

Again, any man who has sons boots them out of the house the moment they turn thirteen and refuses to feed them at the family table. For he says that they are now old enough to feed themselves and trade at a profit as he himself did. And he gives each son twenty or twenty-four groats, or coins to that value, to bargain with and make a profit. The fathers do this so that the sons become practised and quick-witted in all their actions and accustomed to doing business. And this is exactly what happens; for the boys never stop running to and fro all day long, buying this and that and then selling it. When the pearl fishery is in full swing they run down to the port and buy five or six pearls from the fishermen, or as many as they can get. Then they take them to the dealers, who stay indoors for fear of the sun, and say, 'Do you want these? This is what they cost me, for real; let me have whatever profit you think fit.' And the dealers allow them some profit on top of the cost price. Then the boys run off again; or else they say to the dealers, 'Would you like me to go and buy something?' And in this way they become very able and very crafty traders. They still take groceries home for their mothers to cook and prepare for them, but this does not mean they eat anything at their father's expense.

You should also know that in this kingdom and throughout India the beasts and birds are different from ours – all except one bird, and that is the quail. This bird unmistakably resembles ours, but all the rest are very strange and different. I give you my word that they have bats – these are the birds that fly by night and have no quills or feathers – they have birds of this type as big as goshawks. There are goshawks as black as crows and much bigger than ours; they are good fliers and good hawkers. And let me add something else that is worth recounting. You should know that they feed their horses on cooked meat and rice and many other cooked foods.

Let me further tell you that they have many idols, both male and female, in their monasteries; and many girls are offered to these idols in the following manner. The fact is that their mother and father offer them to the idols of their choosing. Once they have been offered, then whenever the monks belonging to the monastery of the idol require the girls who have been offered to this idol to come to the monastery and entertain the idol, they go without delay; and, singing and dancing, they hold a high-spirited celebration. And there are great numbers of these girls forming huge troupes. Another thing: every month, several times a week, these girls bring food to the idols at the place where they were offered; and I will explain how they bring the food there and in what manner they say the idol has eaten. I can tell you that many of these girls whom I have mentioned prepare dishes of meat and other choice ingredients and take them to their idols in the monasteries. Then they spread a table before him with all the dishes they have brought and leave them there for some time. Meanwhile all these girls sing and dance non-stop and lay on the finest entertainment in the world. And when they have kept up this entertainment for as long as it would take a great baron to enjoy a leisurely meal, the girls say that the spirit of the idol has eaten the substance of the food. Then they gather it up and eat it all themselves with great relish and great gaiety. Afterwards they return to their homes. These girls carry on in this way until they get married. And there are plenty of girls like these throughout the kingdom, doing all the things I have told you about.

Why do they lay on these entertainments for the idols? Because the priests who serve the idols often declare, 'The god is angry with the goddess; they refuse to come together or speak to one another. So long as they are bad-tempered and angry and until they are reconciled and make their peace, all our affairs will be undone and will go from bad to worse because they will not bestow their blessing and favour.' And so the aforementioned girls go to the monastery in the way we have said, completely naked apart from covering their private parts, and sing before the god and goddess. The god stands by himself on an altar under a canopy, the goddess by herself on another altar under another canopy; the people say that he often takes his pleasure with her and they have intercourse together, but when they are angry they refrain from intercourse. This is when these girls come to placate them; and when they arrive they set about singing, dancing, leaping, tumbling and performing all sorts of diversions liable to cheer up the god and goddess and reconcile them. While they are performing they say, 'O Lord, why are you angry with the goddess and hard-hearted towards her? Is she not beautiful? Is she not delightful? May it please you therefore to be reconciled with her and take your pleasure with her, for she is unquestionably most delightful.' Then the girl who has spoken these words will lift her leg above her neck and perform a pirouette for the pleasure of the god and goddess. And when they have done enough coaxing they go home. In the morning the priest of the idols will announce as a great blessing that he has seen the god and goddess together and that harmony is restored between them. And then everyone rejoices and gives thanks.

So long as these girls remain virgins, their flesh is so firm that no one can grasp them or pinch them anywhere on their bodies. For a penny they will let a man try to pinch them as hard as he can. After they are married their flesh remains firm, but not as firm as before. Owing to this firmness their breasts do not hang down but stand pertly and conspicuously erect.

The men have very light cane beds fashioned in such a way that when they are in bed and want to go to sleep they can hoist themselves with ropes up to the ceiling and suspend themselves there. They do this in order to escape the aforementioned tarantulas, which have a nasty bite, as well as fleas and other vermin; and also to catch the breeze and combat the heat. Not all do this, though; only the nobles and heads of houses. The rest sleep in the streets. And we will tell you, apropos of the excellent justice kept by the king, that when a man is travelling by night (for on account of the lower temperatures they make their journeys by night rather than day) and wishes to sleep, he will, if he has a sack of pearls or other valuables, put the sack under his head and sleep where he is; and no one ever loses anything by theft or otherwise. And if he does lose something, he is reimbursed without delay – provided, that is, that he has slept on the road, because if he has slept away from the road he gets nothing. In fact he is presumed guilty. For the authorities say, 'Why would you have slept off the road unless you intended to rob others?' So he is punished and his loss is not made good.

We have now told you a great deal about the customs and manners and affairs of this kingdom. So we will leave it and move on to tell you about another kingdom, whose name is Motupalli.

Motupalli is a kingdom reached by travelling north from Maabar for about 1,000 miles. It belongs to a queen who is a woman of great wisdom. For let me tell you that it was a good forty years since the king her husband had died – a husband to whom she had been so deeply devoted that she declared God would never wish her to take another when he whom she had loved more than herself was dead. So for this reason she never sought to marry again. You may take my word for it that throughout her forty-year reign this queen has ruled her kingdom with great justice and great integrity, just as her husband did before her. And I assure you that she is more dearly loved by her subjects than any lady or lord has ever been.

The people are idolaters and pay tribute to no one. They live on rice, meat, milk, fish and fruit.

Diamonds are also produced in this kingdom, and we will tell you how. You should know that in this kingdom there are many mountains in which diamonds are found, as you will hear. For you should know that when it rains the water rushes down through these mountains, cascading wildly along vast ravines and caverns. And when the rain has stopped and the water has drained away the men head out into the ravines through which the water flowed in search of diamonds, which they find in plenty. In summer, when there is not a drop of water to be found here, they uncover plenty of them in the mountains themselves. The heat, though, is so intense as to be all but intolerable. And let me tell you that these mountains are so heavily infested with great fat serpents that men cannot go there without fearing for their lives. But all the same they make their way as best they can and find some very fine, large diamonds. I can also tell you that these serpents are highly venomous and vicious, so the men do not dare enter the caves where these vicious serpents live. And again I can tell you that the men extract the diamonds by other means. You should know that there are great, deep valleys whose rocky sides are so steep that no one can penetrate them. But I will tell you what the men do. They take some lumps of bloody meat and fling them down into the depths of the valleys; and the places where the meat is flung are littered with diamonds, which become embedded in the flesh. Now the fact is that many white eagles live among these mountains and prey on the serpents. And when these eagles see the meat lying at the bottom of the valleys, they swoop down, seize the lumps and carry them off. The men, meanwhile, have been carefully watching where the eagles go, and as soon as they see that one has alighted and is swallowing the meat they rush over as fast as they can. The eagles are so fearful of the men who have surprised them that they fly off and fail to take away the meat. And when the men reach the place where the meat is, they pick it up and find it studded with diamonds.

The men also get hold of the diamonds in the following way. When the eagles eat the meat I have told you about, they also eat – or rather swallow – some of the diamonds. And at night, when they return to their nests, they pass the diamonds they have swallowed along with their faecal matter. Then the men arrive and collect the eagle's excrement, which also turns out to be rich in diamonds.

You have now heard three ways in which diamonds are gathered; there are many others besides. And you should know that diamonds are not found anywhere else in the world but in this kingdom alone. Here, though, they are both plentiful and of fine quality. And do not imagine that the best diamonds find their way to our Christian countries; on the contrary, they are taken to the Great Khan and the kings and barons of these various regions and realms. For they have the greatest treasures, and they buy all the costliest stones.

Now I have told you about the diamonds, so we will move on to other matters. You should know that this kingdom produces the best-quality buckrams – the finest, most beautiful and most valuable in the world. For I assure you that they resemble the linen fabrics of Rheims. There is not a king or queen in the world who would not gladly wear a fabric of such magnificence and beauty.

They have plenty of beasts, including the biggest sheep in the world. They are amply and richly endowed with all the means of life.

There is nothing else worth mentioning, so we will leave this kingdom and tell you about the burial place of Messer St Thomas the Apostle.

The body of Messer St Thomas the Apostle lies in a little town in the province of Maabar. There are few inhabitants, and merchants do not visit the place because it has no merchandise worth taking away and because it is in a very out-of-the-way spot. Yet the fact is that many Christians and many Muslims make pilgrimages to this place. For I can tell you that the Muslims of this country have great faith in him and declare that he was a Muslim; they say he was a great prophet and call him *avariun*, which means 'holy man'.

The Christians who guard the church have many trees that yield wine and bear coconuts. One of these nuts provides enough food and drink to make a meal for a man. They have first an outer husk covered, so to speak, with threads; these are used in all sorts of ways and serve many useful purposes. Inside this husk there is a type of food that provides a square meal for a man. It is really very tasty, as sweet as sugar and white as milk, and is formed in the shape of a cup like the surrounding husk. At the centre of this edible layer there is enough water to fill a flask. It is clear and cool and tastes delicious, and is drunk after eating the flesh. And so from one nut a man has his fill of both food and drink. For each of these trees the Christians pay one groat a month to one of the brothers who are kings in the province of Maabar.

You should also know that a marvel such as I will describe happens here. Now let me tell you that the Christians who come here on pilgrimage gather some of the earth from the place where the saint was killed and take it back to their own country. If anyone falls ill with a quartan or tertian ague or some such fever, they give him a potion made with a little of this earth; and no sooner has the sick man drunk it than he is cured. And every sick person who has drunk this earth has likewise been cured. Messer Marco took some of this earth with him to Venice and cured many people with it. And you should know that this earth is red.

Let me tell you, too, about a fine miracle that happened around the year 1288 from the incarnation of Christ. The fact is that a baron of this country had a vast quantity of the grain they call rice, and he filled up all the houses around the church with it. When the Christians who guard the church and the saint's body saw that this idolatrous baron was filling up the houses in this way and that the pilgrims would have nowhere to lodge, they were deeply distressed and earnestly begged him to desist. But he, being a cruel and haughty man, paid no heed to their prayers and filled up all these houses in accordance with his own wishes and contrary to the wishes of the Christians who guard the church. And when to the fury of the brethren this baron had filled up all the houses of St Thomas with his rice, the great miracle that I will tell you about took place. For you should know that the night after the baron had had these houses filled up, Messer St Thomas the Apostle appeared to him with a fork in his hand and held it to the baron's throat, calling him by name and saying to him, 'If you do not have my houses emptied immediately,

you will die a terrible death.' As he said these words
he pressed the fork hard against the throat of the
baron, who was convinced he was in great pain and
all but certain he was dying. And when Messer
St Thomas had done this he went away. In the morning the baron arose early and had all the houses
emptied. And he related everything that Messer
St Thomas had done to him, which was held to be a
great miracle. The Christians were filled with joy and
gladness at it, and they repeatedly rendered great
thanks and great honour to Messer St Thomas and
profusely blessed his name. And I assure you that
many other miracles happen here all year round
which would undoubtedly be reckoned great marvels
by anyone who heard of them – above all the healing
of Christians who are lame or disabled.

Now that we have told you about this, we also want
to tell you how St Thomas was killed according to
the people of these parts. The fact is that Messer
St Thomas was outside his hermitage in the woods,
praying to the Lord his God. Around him were many
peacocks, for you should know that in this country
they are more common than anywhere else in the
world. And while Messer St Thomas was at prayer an

idolater of the lineage and race of the *gavi* let fly an arrow from his bow, intending to kill one of the peacocks that were gathered around the saint. He never even saw the saint; but instead of hitting the peacock as he thought, he had hit Messer St Thomas the Apostle in the middle of his right side. When he had received this blow he worshipped his creator with great gentleness; and I can tell you it was from this blow that he died. But it is a fact that before he came to this place where he died he made many converts in Nubia. As to the ways and means by which this came about, we will set it all out clearly for you in this book at the proper time and place.

Now we have told you about St Thomas, so we will move on to tell you about other things.

The fact is that when a child is born here they anoint him once a week with sesame oil, and this turns him a great deal darker than when he was born. For let me tell you that the blackest men here are held in highest regard and considered superior to those who are not so black. And I will tell you another thing, too. You may take my word for it that these people portray and paint all their gods and idols black and their devils white as snow. For they say that God and all the saints are black – speaking, of course, of their God and their saints – and that the devils are white. And so they portray and paint them in the way you have heard; and I can tell you that the statues they make of their idols are likewise all black.

You should also know that the men of this country have such faith in the ox and such belief in its sanctity that when they go to war they take with them some of the hair of the wild oxen I told you about before; those who are horsemen tie some of this ox hair to their horse's mane, while the foot soldiers fasten some of the ox hair to their shields or in some cases knot it on to their own hair. And they do this because they believe that this ox hair will help protect and save them from all kinds of danger. Everyone who joins the army follows suit. And you should know that for this reason the hair of the wild ox is worth a good deal here; for if a man has none he does not feel safe.

Since we have told you about this matter we will move on and tell you about a province of the Brahmins, as you will be able to hear.

Lar is a province that lies to the west of the place where St Thomas the Apostle is buried. All the

Brahmins in the world are sprung from this province, for this is where they originated. Let me tell you that these Brahmins are among the best and most trustworthy traders in the world; for they would not tell a lie for anything in the world or speak a word that was not true. You should know that if a foreign merchant who knows nothing of the manners and customs of these parts comes to this province to do business, he finds one of these Brahmins and entrusts him with his money and goods, asking him to conduct his business on his behalf lest he should be deceived through ignorance of the local customs. The Brahmin merchant promptly takes charge of the foreign merchant's goods and, when both selling and buying, deals with them as scrupulously and promotes the foreigner's interests at least as carefully as if he were acting for himself. In return for this service he asks for nothing, leaving any recompense to the foreigner's goodwill.

They do not eat meat or drink wine. They live very virtuous lives by their own lights. They do not have sex with any women except their wives. They would never take anything that belonged to someone else, or kill an animal, or do anything they believed might lead them to sin. I can also tell you that all Brahmins are known by an emblem they wear. For you should know that all the Brahmins in the world sling a cotton cord over one shoulder and tie it under the opposite arm, so that the cord crosses both the chest and back. And wherever they go they are known by this emblem. I can further tell you that they have a king who is mightily rich in treasure. This king is an enthusiastic purchaser of pearls and every other kind of precious stone. In fact he has struck a deal with all the merchants of his country that for all the pearls they bring him from the kingdom of Maabar known as Chola – which is the wealthiest and most sophisticated province in India and the source of the finest pearls – he will give them double the purchase price. So the Brahmins go to the kingdom of Maabar and buy up all the fine pearls they can find and take them to their king, declaring on their honour what they cost. And the king promptly has them paid double the cost price; not once have they received less than that. Thanks to this they have brought him enormous quantities of very fine, large pearls.

These Brahmins are idolaters who set more store by augury and the behaviour of beasts and birds than any other men in the world. So I will tell you a bit about what they do in this regard, beginning with a particular custom that is observed among them. The fact is that they have allotted a sign to every day of the week, as I will explain. If it happens that they are bargaining over some piece of merchandise, the prospective buyer stands up and examines his shadow in the sunlight, saying, 'What day is it today? Such-and-such a day.' Then he has his shadow measured. If it is the right length for that day, he makes the purchase; if it is not the length it should be, he absolutely does not make the purchase but rather waits till the shadow has reached the point laid down in their rule. Just as I have told you with respect to this day, so they have laid down the length the shadow ought to be on every day of the week; and until the shadow has reached the desired length they will not conduct any bargain or any other business. But when the shadow reaches the desired length for the day, they conclude all their bargains and business.

I will tell you something even more remarkable. Say they are in the middle of striking a bargain – whether indoors or out – and they see a tarantula approaching, these being very common here. If the purchaser sees it coming from a direction that seems auspicious to him, he will buy the goods without delay; but if the tarantula does not come from a direction he believes to be auspicious, he will call off the deal and abandon the purchase.

I can also tell you that if they are leaving their house when they hear someone sneeze and they decide it is not propitious, they will stop and go no further. And here is another thing. Say these Brahmins are going on their way when they see a swallow flying towards them, whether from ahead or from the left or right. If it appears according to their beliefs that the swallow comes from an auspicious direction, then they will go ahead; but if it appears to come from an inauspicious direction, then they will go no further but turn back.

These Brahmins live longer than any other people in the world; this is due to their sparse diet and strict abstinence. They have very healthy teeth thanks to a herb they chew with their meals, which is a great aid to digestion and very wholesome for the human body. And you should know that these Brahmins do not practise bloodletting, either from the veins or from any other part of the body.

Among them are some men living under a rule who are called *yogis*. They live even longer than the others, for they reach 150 to 200 years of age. Yet they remain so physically fit that they can still come and go wherever they want and perform all the necessary services for their monastery and idols, serving them just as well as if they were younger. This comes of the strict abstinence they practise by eating small portions of healthy food; for their customary diet consists chiefly of rice and milk. And I can further tell you that these *yogi* who live to the great age I have mentioned also ingest the following substance, which will surely strike you as an extraordinary thing. For I assure you that they take quicksilver and sulphur and mix them together to make a drink, which they then swallow. They say it prolongs life, and so they live all the longer. I can tell you that they take it twice a month. You should know, too, that these people start taking this drink from childhood in order to live longer. And certainly those who live to the age I have mentioned take this drink of sulphur and quicksilver.

There is also a religious order in this kingdom of Maabar of those called *yogi*. They carry abstinence to the extremes I will describe and lead a harsh and austere life. For you may take my word for it that they go stark naked and entirely unclothed, with their private parts and every other part of their bodies uncovered. They worship the ox, and most of them wear a miniature ox made of gilt copper or bronze in the middle of their foreheads; you understand that these are tied in place. I can also tell you that they burn ox dung and make a powder of it. Then they anoint various parts of their body with it, showing great reverence – at least as much as Christians do when using holy water. And if anyone salutes them in the street, they anoint his forehead with this pow- der as if it were the holiest of actions. They do not eat from bowls or trenchers; instead they take their food on the leaves of apples of paradise or other large leaves, but only when they are dried and no longer green. For they say that green leaves have souls and so it would be sinful. And let me tell you that they guard against acting towards any living creature in a way they believe will give rise to sin; for the fact is they would sooner die than do anything they deem sinful. When other men ask them why they go naked and are not ashamed to show their members, they reply, 'We go naked because we want nothing of this world; for we came into the world naked and unclothed. As for not being ashamed to show our members, the fact is that we do no sin with them and therefore have no more shame in them than you have when you show your hand or face or the other parts of your body that do not lead you into carnal sin; whereas you use your members to commit sin and lechery, and so you cover them up and are ashamed of them. But we are no more ashamed of showing them than we are of showing our fingers, because we do not sin with them.' This is the explanation they give to men who ask them why they are not ashamed to show their members. Again, I assure you they would never kill any creature or living thing on earth – be it a fly, flea, louse or any other kind of vermin – because they say they have souls. This, they say, is why they would never eat them; for if they did they would commit a sin. I can also tell you that they never eat anything green, be it herb or root, until it has been dried; for they say that green things have souls. When they wish to void their bowels, they go down to the beach or seashore and relieve themselves on the sand near the water's edge. When they are done they wash themselves thoroughly in the water, and when they are clean they take a little rod or twig and use it to flatten out their excrement, spreading it this way and that across the sand until no trace of it can be seen. When asked why they do this, they reply, 'Because it would breed worms, and when the sun dried out their source of nourishment, these worms that had been created would die for want of food; and since this substance emanates from our body (for we, too, cannot live without food) we would be committing a very grave sin by bringing about the death of so many souls that would have sprung from our substance. So we destroy this substance in such a way that worms cannot possibly be born from it only to die soon afterwards for want of food through our faults and failings.' And another thing: I can tell you that they sleep stark naked on the ground without a stitch to cover them or to lie on. It is quite astonishing that they do not die but rather live to the great age I mentioned above.

They are the most abstemious eaters, for they fast all year round and drink nothing but water.

I will tell you another thing about them, too. Among them are monks who live in monasteries to serve their idols. And when they are named to a new office or rank – for instance, if someone dies and his replacement needs to be chosen – they are put to the test in the following way. The girls who have been offered to the idols are brought in and made to touch the men who tend to the idols. They caress them in this place and that all over their bodies, embracing and kissing them and bringing them to the utmost pitch of earthly pleasure. If a man is fondled in this way by the girls I have told you about and his member does not in the least react but rather stays just as it was before the girls touched him, he passes muster and stays in the monastery. But if another man is fondled by the girls and his member reacts and grows erect, far from retaining him they drive him away at once, declaring that they cannot stand having a lecher among them. This is how cruel and false-hearted these idolaters are.

The reason they give for burning their dead is this. They say that if they did not burn the corpse it would breed worms, and after the worms had eaten the body from which they sprang they would have nothing left to eat and would perforce die. And they say that if the worms were to die the soul of the deceased would incur great sin. So this is the reason they give for

43

burning their dead. And they say that worms have souls.

Now we have told you about the customs of these idolaters, so we will take our leave of them and tell you a delightful story that slipped our mind when we were dealing with the island of Ceylon. You will hear it for yourselves, and it will surely fill you with wonder.

Ceylon, as I told you earlier in this book, is a big island. Now the fact is that on this island there is a very high mountain, so precipitous and rocky that no one can climb it except in the way I will now tell you. For many iron chains are hung from the side of the mountain, so arranged that men can use them to climb to the summit. Now let me tell you this: it is said that on the top of this mountain is the monument of Adam, our first father. The Muslims say it is Adam's grave; the idolaters, though, say it is the monument of Sakyamuni Burkhan.

This Sakyamuni was the first man in whose name idols were made. For by their lights he was the best man who ever lived among them, and he was the first whom they revered as a saint and in whose name they made idols. He was the son of a great king who was both rich and powerful. And he – the son – was so pure of mind that he paid no heed to worldly affairs and did not wish to be king. When his father saw that he had no wish to be king and had no interest in worldly affairs, he was deeply troubled. So he made him a very generous offer: he said he would crown him king of the realm and that he could rule it at his pleasure. Moreover he was willing to resign the crown and issue no commands whatsoever, so that his son would be the sole ruler. His son replied that he wanted nothing. And when his father saw that nothing in the world would tempt him to accept the kingship, he was so deeply distressed that he came close to dying of grief. And no wonder; for he had no other son and no one else to whom he could leave his kingdom. So the king took the following course of action. He resolved to find a way to make his son willingly embrace worldly affairs and accept the crown and the kingdom. So he moved him into an exquisite palace and gave him 30,000 ravishing and captivating girls to serve him; not a single man was admitted but only these girls. And girls put him to bed and served him at table and kept him company all day long. They sang and danced for him and did everything they could to divert him, just as the king had commanded. Yet I can tell you that all these girls could not do enough to awaken any sexual appetites in the king's son; on the contrary, he lived more strictly and chastely than before and led a very virtuous life by their lights. I should also tell you that he was brought up so fastidiously that he had never left the palace nor seen a dead man or anyone who was not able-bodied, for his father had not let anyone old or infirm into his presence. Now it happened one day that this young man was riding along the road when he saw a dead body. He was quite horrified, as someone would be if they had never seen one before, and immediately asked his companions what it was. They told him it was a dead man. 'What,' said the king's son, 'do all men then die?' 'Indeed they do,' they replied. At this the young man fell silent and rode on deep in thought. He had not ridden far when he came across an ancient man who could not walk and had no teeth in his mouth, having lost them all through extreme old age. And when the king's son saw the old man he asked what he was and why he could not walk. His companions told him it was owing to old age that he could not walk and it was owing to old age that he had lost his teeth. And when the king's son had digested the truth about the dead man and the old man, he went back to his palace and resolved to remain no longer in this evil world but to set out in search of him who never dies and who had created him. And so he abandoned his palace and his father. He headed among vast, remote mountains and spent the rest of his days there, leading a life of virtue, chastity and great abstemiousness. If he had been a Christian he would undoubtedly be a great saint and dwell with our Lord Jesus Christ.

When this prince died, his body was brought to the king his father. And when the king saw that the son whom he loved more than himself was dead, there is no need to ask whether he was afflicted and grief-stricken. First he mourned deeply. Then he had an image made in his likeness, entirely of gold and precious stones, and had it honoured by all the people of the land and worshipped as a god. And they say that he died eighty-four times. For they say that the first time he died he became an ox, and the second time he died he became a horse. In this way they say he died eighty-four times, each time becoming a dog or another sort of animal until the eighty-fourth time, when they say he died and became a god. And the idolaters hold him to be the best and the greatest of their gods. You should know that this was the first idol the idolaters had, and all the idols derive from him. And this happened in the island of Ceylon in India.

Now you have heard how the idols originated. And I give you my word that the idolaters come here on pilgrimage from very distant parts, just as Christians make pilgrimages to the shrine of Messer St James. The idolaters say that the monument on this mountain is that of the king's son of whom you have heard, and that the teeth and the hair and the bowl that are kept here also belonged to this prince, whose name was Sakyamuni Burkhan, which means St Sakyamuni. But the Muslims, who also come here in great numbers on pilgrimage, say it is the monument of Adam, our first father, and that the teeth and hair and bowl also belonged to Adam. So now you have heard how the idolaters say he is the king's son who was their first idol and their first god, and how the Muslims say he is Adam, our first father. But God alone knows who he is and what he was. For we do not believe that Adam is in this place, since our Scripture of Holy Church says that he is in another part of the world.

Now it happened that the Great Khan heard that the monument of Adam was on this mountain, along with his teeth and his hair and the bowl from which he ate. He made up his mind that he must have the teeth and the bowl and the hair. So he sent a great embassy here in the year 1284 from the incarnation of Christ. What else shall I tell you? You may be quite certain that the Great Khan's messengers set out with a vast retinue and journeyed so far by land and sea that they came to the island of Ceylon. They went to the king and made such great efforts that they acquired two great big molar teeth as well as some of the hair and the bowl. The bowl was made of exquisite green porphyry. And when the Great Khan's messengers had these items I have mentioned in their possession, they set off and made their way back to their lord. When they were near the great city of Khanbaliq where the Great Khan was residing, they sent him word that they were coming and were bringing the things he had sent them for. At this the Great Khan ordered all the people, both the monks and the others, to go out and meet these relics, which they were given to understand belonged to Adam. But why make a long story of it? You may well believe that all the people of Khanbaliq went out to meet the relics; and the monks received them and brought them to the Great Khan, who accepted them with great joy and great ceremony and great reverence. And let me tell you that they found in their scriptures a passage declaring that the bowl possessed this property: that if food for one man were put inside, it would provide enough to feed five. And the Great Khan announced that he had put this to the proof and that it was quite true.

This is how the Great Khan came by these relics you have heard about; and undoubtedly the treasure it cost him to obtain them amounted to a substantial sum.

Now that we have told you this whole story in due order, with all the facts, we will move on and tell you about other things. And first of all we will tell you about the city of Kayal.

Kayal is a great and splendid city that belongs to Ashar, the eldest of the five royal brothers. And you

may take my word for it that this is the port of call
for all shipping coming from the west – that is, from
Hormuz and Kish and Aden and all Arabia – laden
with horses and other goods. The merchants use this
city's port because it is conveniently situated and
offers a good market for their wares, and also because
merchants from many parts congregate here to buy
merchandise and horses and other things. The king
is very rich in treasure; he adorns his person with
many valuable gems and goes about in great state.
He governs his kingdom ably and maintains a high
standard of justice, especially in the case of the merchants who come here from other parts – that is, the
foreign merchants. He watches over their interests
with great integrity. And the merchants, I assure you,
are very glad to come here on account of this good
king who looks after them so well. And it is certainly
true that they make huge profits here and their business prospers.

I will also tell you that this king has at least
300 wives; for the more wives a man keeps here, the
greater his honour is held to be. And I can tell you,
too, that when a quarrel breaks out between these
five kings (who are brothers-german born of the same

father and mother) and they are determined to declare
war on one another, then their mother, who is still
alive, intervenes between them and refuses to let them
fight. If, as often happens, her sons will not heed her
prayers but are determined to defy her and fight, then
their mother seizes a knife and cries, 'If you do not
stop quarrelling and make peace with one another,
I will kill myself here and now. And first of all I will
cut from my bosom the breasts with which I gave you
my milk.' And when the sons see how deeply their
mother is grieved and how tenderly she pleads with
them, and reflect that it is for their own good, they
come to terms and make peace. This has happened
time after time. Even so, I can tell you that after their
mother's death an almighty quarrel will unavoidably
break out among them and they will destroy one
another.

You should also know that the people of this city,
as of India as a whole, have the following custom:
out of habit and for the pleasure it gives them, they
almost constantly keep in their mouths a kind of leaf
called *tambur*. They go round chewing this leaf and
spitting out the resulting spittle. And this habit is

especially prevalent among the nobles and magnates and kings. They have these leaves prepared with camphor and other spices and go about continually chewing them; lime is also added to the mix. And this keeps them very healthy. Moreover if anyone wishes to insult and taunt someone who has offended him, then when he meets him in the street he collects this mixture in his mouth and spits it in the other's face, saying, 'You are not worth this', referring to what he has spat out. The other, regarding this as a gross affront and insult, promptly complains to the king that so-and-so has slighted and abused him and asks the king's leave to avenge himself. To be precise, if the assailant has insulted him and his clan, he will ask leave to pit himself against the assailant and his clan against the assailant's clan until he has proved whether or not he is worth no more than that. But if it is a purely personal insult, he will ask leave to settle it man to man. Then the king grants leave to both parties. If it is to be a battle of the clans, each man gets ready for the fight with his own people; and the only armour they don and wear for protection is the skin their mothers gave them when they were born.

When they are on the field and battle commences they strike, wound and kill one another, for their swords easily pierce their skin and they are all easy targets. The king will be present with a multitude of people to watch the proceedings; and when he sees that large numbers have been killed on both sides and that one side seems to have the upper hand and is overwhelming the other, he will take one end of the cloth he has wrapped round him and put it between his teeth, then hold out the other end at arm's length. At this the combatants will immediately stop fighting without striking another blow. And this is often how it turns out. If the combat is man to man they will both be naked, just as they are normally, and each will have a knife. They are very skilled at defending themselves with these knives, for they are adept at parrying a blow with them as well as attacking their opponent. This, then, is the procedure. As you have gathered, they are dark-skinned people. So one of them will draw a white circle wherever he chooses on the other's body, saying to him, 'Know that I will strike you in this circle and nowhere else; defend yourself as best you can.' And the other will do the same to him. Lucky for him who fares better, unlucky for him who fares worse; for whenever one of them strikes the other he feels it sharply enough.

[. . .]

Gujarat is also a large kingdom. The people are idolaters and have a king and their own language; they pay tribute to no one. The kingdom lies towards the west. And from here the Pole Star is still more clearly visible, for it appears at an altitude of at least six cubits. This kingdom is home to the most infamous pirates in the world. And I assure you that they perpetrate the enormity I will now describe. For you should know that when these wicked pirates capture merchants they make them drink tamarind mixed with seawater, which sends the merchants scurrying below to pass or vomit up the contents of their stomachs. The pirates then collect everything the merchants have produced and sift through it to see if it contains any pearls or other precious stones. For the pirates say that when the merchants are captured they swallow their pearls and other precious stones to keep them out of their captors' hands. And so these wicked pirates give the merchants this drink for the malicious purpose I have told you about.

They have huge quantities of pepper; they also have plenty of ginger and a great deal of indigo. They have plenty of cotton, too, for the trees that produce cotton grow here to a great height – as much as six paces after twenty years' growth. In truth when the trees reach this age they no longer produce cotton fit for spinning; instead it is used for wadding and quilting. And this is the rule with these trees: up to twelve years they produce fine cotton for spinning, but from twelve to twenty the cotton they produce is not as good as when they were young.

Immense quantities of skins are made into leather in this kingdom: that is, they tan the hides of goats, buffaloes, wild oxen, unicorns and many other beasts. I assure you they are tanned on such a scale that every year numerous ships load up with them and set sail for Arabia and many other parts; for this kingdom supplies many other kingdoms and provinces. I can also tell you that in this kingdom they make beautiful red leather mats embossed with birds and beasts and exquisitely embroidered with gold and silver thread. They are so beautiful that they are a marvel to behold. You should understand that these leather mats I am telling you about are used by the Muslims to sleep on; and how well you sleep on them! They also make cushions here, embroidered with gold and so beautiful that they are worth at least six silver marks. And some of the mats I have told you about are worth at least ten silver marks. What else shall I tell you? You may depend on it that in this kingdom they make the most finely crafted leather goods in the world, and the most expensive.

Now that we have given you all the facts about this kingdom in due order, we will go on our way . . .